Beso
the Donkey

Beso
the Donkey

POEMS BY

Richard Jarrette

MICHIGAN STATE UNIVERSITY PRESS ▪ *East Lansing*

♾ The paper used in this publication meets the minimum requirements of ANSI/NISO
Z39.48-1992 (R 1997) (Permanence of Paper).

 Michigan State University Press
East Lansing, Michigan 48823-5245

Printed and bound in the United States of America.

18   17   16   15   14   13   12   11   10   1   2   3   4   5   6   7   8   9   10

LIBRARY OF CONGRESS CATALOGING-IN-PUBLICATION DATA
Jarrette, Richard.
Beso the donkey : poems / Richard Jarrette.
p. cm.
ISBN 978-0-87013-979-6 (pbk. : alk. paper)
I. Title.
PS3610.A776B47 2010
811'.6—dc22
2010003513

Cover design by Erin Kirk New
Book design by Charlie Sharp, Sharp Des!gns, Lansing, Michigan

g green   Michigan State University Press is a member of the Green Press Initiative
  press   and is committed to developing and encouraging ecologically responsible
  INITIATIVE
publishing practices. For more information about the Green Press Initiative and the use
of recycled paper in book publishing, please visit *www.greenpressinitiative.org.*

Visit Michigan State University Press on the World Wide Web at
www.msupress.msu.edu

for Ekaterina Galiyeva, RN

CONTENTS

II. With Beso

III. Beyond Beso

‖

Preface

Attending Beso

*Unto all mortals let
there be equal grace.*
—Buddhist prayer

I attend to Beso,
a donkey who will die
but asks so little of me,
a grave and painful enigma.
I inquire with my heart—
he nods with the nobility
of a bearded oak,
or Solomon.

I. Beso

The Monumental Beso

The Lord made a hill.
Beso wandered to the top
and with the shape of his body,
a nose in the grass, and tall ears,
said, *I am a donkey.*

We can celebrate this miracle
with a monument—a hill
climbed by Beso the Donkey,
every so often, in mild weather
when the grass is green.

Certain Beso

Beso crossed the river
of ground fog at dawn
to rub his forehead
on a post.

He's becoming certain
which branch
among ten thousand willows
upholds

the mourning dove.

Beso's Equanimity

He studies cabbage butterflies, bees
gathered on the rim of his water
bucket, and birds feasting on a sudden
blizzard of downy thistle seeds.

I believe that when evil fell upon
Beso, that he regarded it with the same
equanimity and complained loudly,
kicked, and bit the demon.

Beso's Hooves

He tracks the plowing
a mile away with his left ear
but does not look.

Beso's hooves have known
roads twisted like sheeps' guts
and bad weather.

> *And what with broken wheels and so on,*
> *I won't say it wasn't hard going,*
> *Over roads twisted like sheeps' guts.*
> —Ezra Pound, "Exile's Letter"

Beside Beso

Beso's coat is a forest of ears and nerves,
each hair sensitive as the eyelash
of a hummingbird.

My hand on his back—a boil of flies
tasting rigging scars.

He'll drift away if he senses a load
like an untethered skiff in the shadows
under a dock.

Beso the Donkey

Beso the Donkey
lives out his days in a small pasture.
He appears stoic in the rain
and stands still
beneath the merciless sun.
You could almost believe that a rock
to eat, dust to drink,
are all that he needs.
You would be more wrong
than the one who named him *Beso*
thinking that the kiss he gave
for a sliver of apple
was love.

Beso's Song

... you built temples for them
in their hearing.

—Rainer Maria Rilke

Beso was damaged,
thrown away.
I would cover my ears
and weep,
bent with grief,
if he began to sing
like Orpheus.
Would it still be
a human being,
swollen with hearing,
that survived his song?

To Comfort Beso

I wish to comfort Beso
but often fail.

He runs from me
as if I am coming to brand
him with the map
of my life.

Beso's Fence

Beso does not seem to get angry
at the fence.
He stops, looks over,
sticks his head through to reach
some thistles, taste a shoe—
licks and carefully bites the boards
after reading each one
with his nose like braille—
investigates every splinter and knot
more than once.

Wild Beso

Beso snorts and grunts,
almost a growl,
when he spots the dry grass
in my fist
and gives me a look
as if expecting
wild buttercups.
Last night he prevailed against
mountain lion, Draco,
loneliness?

Beso the Jack

Beso evades me to study
the southwest gate.

I think he wishes I was an ass,
a jenny broadcasting pheromones
wrapped in the menthol
of Point Sal Sage.

He reads the mood of my hand
through the brush—
the argument still raging
with my first wife,
the melting tenderness
when my granddaughter says,
I miss you Papa, into
the telephone.

He's assessing my frailties
in case I get in his way.

Husk Beso

I fear Beso.

His ancestors read lions,
hyenas, skillful men,
and worked out the escape,
or counterattack, as a herd
with snorts and stomps.

I touch Beso's body
and feel the weathered lumber
of a long abandoned barn—
rusted tools inside, tractor,
two owls.

His mind may have fled
deranging solitude
too far
harrowing empty grasslands
for the others.

I attend the husk of a jackass,
quiet as a landmine,
who could bolt from his nightmare
and kill unwise dog,
horse, or man.

A Paradise for Beso

One of the scars on Beso's back
squirms under my hand like a snake
trying to free itself from a bag.

His head will snap around to bite
if I forget that he can't forget.

I pray for him to awaken in paradise—
no flies, no leather, and nothing
with hands.

Dear Beso

If I can learn to gently
file your teeth,
keep the bucket full,
feed you well,
and care
for your hooves,
may I be your companion
in idleness?
I do not expect you
to believe
that I want nothing
in return.

Beso Follows

Beso drifts to the fence
and watches crows
forage for bugs and worms
after the plowing.

He seems to follow
how they turn over leaves
and clods with their beaks.

His ears are busy
tracking the entire flock, and drips
resonating from a tin
downspout.

Beso Attends

The waxing moon
bends its bow toward
Venus in the west.

Beso carries the stars
on his back
and one in each eye.

Crickets fill the soft
night air
with love songs.

When they suddenly stop
he startles and fully
attends to why.

Cézanne and Beso

When I lift my head from the desk,
Beso is at my window.

It was said of Cézanne
that he could look at things like a dog,
like the first human being to put
his hand on the earth.

Beso can look at a man
like a donkey—one ear turned to me
the other to howling coyotes.

Bach Beso

I look at Beso as he regards
Bach's *Cello Suite Number 5
in C Minor* because ass ears,
audience to all that comes
his way, give him no choice.
I wonder what he makes of it—
threat? opportunity? hyenas
feeding in the dark house?

Beso's Window

Blue
Carolina blue
with sun
silvery grays
intense Egyptian
violet
raven black
the Milky Way
Perdita rose
no glass

Beso and His Peers

An unapparent connexion
is stronger than an apparent.
—Heraclitus

Beso and his peers hold
firm to agreements forged
during last night's
congress.

Numberless shadows
run over the butter lettuce
into the vineyard
at first light.

Beso Stomps

Beso studies the dispute
between two red-winged
blackbirds

stomps his left hind hoof
and scares them into
the cabbage

startling a killdeer
who shoots ten feet into the air
launching

Beso's ears.

Al-Beso

Beso rolls in the dirt,
appears satisfied,
and fully attends to me
with both ears from a solid
unaffected stance.

The Lord has reveled
in his creation
and will receive praise.

Brothers and sisters,
forgive me,
the one-hundredth name of God:
Al-Beso, and his world
is sacred.

Beso's Deepest

I am a poor man
whose donkey judges
the water bucket,
forage, and threat.
Beso deposits his
deepest in the pasture
for fervent study
by flies, sun, wind,
the heavens.

Beso's Bucket

A brilliant night—
Beso writes his haiku with
his nose on the stars.

Beso the Acropolis

Suspicious of moon
and Orion, field mice

steal through the pasture
to feast and debate under

the protection of Beso
the Acropolis.

To Touch Beso

If you reach through the fence
to touch Beso,
there's a chance that he will allow you
to stroke his muzzle,
or scratch behind his ears.
People are so happy when he drifts over
and extends his nose,
as if Luciano Pavarotti unexpectedly
opened his door and invited
everyone to join him
for lunch.

Beso's Dignity

I approach Beso
the Donkey
who gazes beyond
with the tragic dignity
of Abraham Lincoln
weathered by grave news.
Today it is: two
hands, one halter,
no apple.

Beso Glared

I stumbled into Beso
who snorted,
stomped his left hind hoof
and glared.

My apology was not
well received.

He drifted off
but came back for one apple
and his favorite beer—
St. Andrew's.

Beso's Position

Maybe I should get a dog
who adores me
instead of this barely
tolerant ass
but I admire the integrity
of his well-reasoned position
on carnivores
and I think he's almost
worked out why
the barnyard is quieter
since Christmas.

Beso Solved

Beso solved the latch
and wandered off.

I followed his trail
to some bright
grass around the leaky
irrigation valve
where he was foraging
in the mud.

I washed his feet
when we got home.

Beso's Part

Swallows are back in their mud
nest above the porch light.

Coils of Ekaterina's strawberry
blonde hair, and Coco the Cat's
brown fur, cradle three white eggs
with reddish speckles.

Wiry strands of Beso the Donkey's
gray coat stiffen the nest cup
along with Mexican feather grass,
rye, and switch grass—all hard to kill

and tough as bareknuckle boxers.

Beso the Sphinx

Coco the Cat is poised between
Beso's forelegs
in the shade of his nose.
You could think they're investigating
windblown cottonwoods
to the northeast
crows, and flycatchers,
or that the goddess Bast
is receiving instructions
between the paws of the Sphinx
to baffle us for another eight
thousand years.

Equus Asinus, Beso—On Blame

Sappho might call this
a terrifying wind

carrying off
him who blames me.

Beso turns his back on it
and farts.

> *May terrifying winds carry off*
> *him who blames me.*
>
> —Sappho

Beso Prefers

Beso does not care about
the weight of my guilt,
he simply does not want me
to climb on his back
and prefers that I also leave
behind my nearly weightless
Mother Mary medallion.

Beso's Stream of Gold

I don't think much escapes
Beso's notice.

He can probably smell the rain
in distant clouds,
weigh the heavy humid air,
and concern himself with the branding
five miles from here.

But I know something that he
does not know—
just before the sun disappears
over the ridge,
it is a stream of gold that pours
from his backlit
silhouette.

Beso Dozed Off

Beso appears to have
dozed off
listening to the progress of gophers
with his feet,
and tracking the wildfire
with his nose,
trying to remember which gate
had the broken latch.

Beso and the Mailman

Beso is tired and old
but will wake up
and travel the pasture
to greet the mailman.

He carefully studies
the mouth of the box being
opened and the hand
feeding it.

I wonder if he remembers
the rum cake
my mother sent to me
last year.

II. With Beso

Mission: to be where I am.
Even in that ridiculous, deadly serious
role—I am the place
where creation is working itself out.

—Tomas Tranströmer, "The Outpost"

Beso the Helmsman

A tide of gray fog floods
the valley floor.

Iron oaks drink their brew
with the dead and loom.

Beso measures deep waves
lifting pasture, hills,
and hemisphere,
with ancient earth legs.

The world seems unhewn.

We were marched onto this ark
a long time ago—

what was I?

Ask Beso

Are you wonderful?
Ask Beso
what he thinks about
the drinking song
he endured
when he carried you home
last night.

I Wish Beso

Old Beso serenely chews a thistle.
He looks like he could eat
the rusty coils of barbed wire
behind the shed, or like a Civil War
veteran who could tell you things
about Chancellorsville.

We are lucky animals can't talk,
I am sorry that I can. Last night—
bar stool arguments about politics.
Today, I am clotted with sadness, dust.
I wish Beso could tell me about Mary,
the Virgin, Our Lady of Sorrows.

Beso Brings Beso

Guilty.

We curse enemies,
call each other fox,
pig, mule, horse's ass,
buddy, and say,

*The guy brings a lot
to the table.*

Rumi even said,

*There is one inside
who walks like Jesus
on the sea.*

Beso brings Beso—
every hair.

The Real Beso

A glass made of water
and full of water.
　　　　　　　—Roberto Juarroz

I study Beso from the porch,
pencil and paper ready,
while he follows his nose.

I set my chessmen on the ocean
replacing each one as it sinks.
I have many.

Beso exhales steam in the pasture—
maybe he'll let me warm my
fingers in a cloud.

Hajj to Beso

Beso has no pilgrimage
to complete himself.

The sun makes its hajj
to Beso and circles him,

circles him with brothers,
sisters, and the moon.

Beso *Is a Sound*

To Beso,
Beso is a sound
that awakens hope
for an apple.

To me,
it is a sweetness
in my mouth
like a candy *Kiss*.

It's only a taste,
but a taste.

Beso's Dialect

Would I know
if Beso spoke?
Maybe he has been
conversing with me
in a dialect that he
assumes I understand
because sometimes
I scratch the ears,
fetch the apple,
or leave him alone,
as requested.

Beso Steps Out

I have drawn a circle
around Beso by thinking,
You are a donkey, here.
He steps out of it freely,
and could I follow?

Where Beso

Night is sheer, generous, a galaxy
drains into the eye of a mouse
without hoping for more.

Beso lives with sun, moon,
no moon, just beyond my grasp.

A killdeer says that my mind is puny,
miserly, forgetful—
the richest man in the world
afraid to give a nickel.

Among owls, wind, the eye of Taurus,
I am the only thing that does not
know where Beso is tonight.

Beso Settles It

Inside my heart
I keep three thousand
prancing chestnut horses.
—Muso Soseki

When I find Beso
in my heart,
the hills spread their wings
and fly a little.
Seeing him in the pasture,
four hooves
on the ground,
settles everything.

Earthly Beso

Become one with
the dusty world.
—Lao Tzu

Dirt bath.

Beso and the dusty
world are one.

He's lit like a Vermeer
in his cloud—

an earthly apotheosis
swelling

to engulf me.

Beso Expands

Beso expands, contracts,
with each breath.

So what? Look—a gnat
swells slightly when it inhales.

Oaks feel a tiny shiver
when a moth sighs.

With Beso

The hovering kestrel,
the blue oak, clouds, air,
sun, kangaroo rats,
Beso the Donkey,
live and die together.
With Beso, breathing
in the pasture, wind riffling
hair, feathers, and grass—
psalms and war stories
vanishing in flames
over black hills.

Civilization Beso

After a good rain,
I can see where Beso lingered in the mud
leaving a deeper record of himself
like a lost civilization.
He regarded the crew harvesting cabbage;
studied rain drops falling
in his bucket;
entertained a visitor at the fence
who may have fed him
a yellow onion;
stood with the blue oak at dusk facing west;
they were joined by a man
and his walking stick.

Beso Engages

You say nothing, so it's
clear enough we share a
kindred mind.
— Po Chü-I

I used to talk to Beso,
run things by him,
say soothing words,
but gradually stopped.
His utter indifference
to my voice sank in.
When we idle together,
he can look through me
for the longest time.

Beso's Jaw

When I accepted grief
as my companion,
I stroked Beso's jaw
and could not name
one enemy.

Beso's Mind

My agreement with gravity
compounds with age.

I dip my nose in the Milky Way
and feel how deep.

I wander far from my head
and its donkey-tying stake.

Mood Beso

Sometimes I forget that I am not a beard
of Spanish moss in the blue oak
and that Beso the Donkey
is not Duke Ellington's *Mood Indigo*.

Wounded Beso

Beso and his old wounds age
far from the wild herd.

I offer gentle brushing
but he pulls away.

The many good things I share
are never enough.

He attends equally to my
kind words and bees.

It's when I don't want anything
that he drifts near.

III. Beyond Beso

May his soul walk under the larches of Paradise.
May his soul walk in the wood there.

Out of the turmoil, Mother of Griefs, receive him,
Queen of Heaven, receive him.

May the sound of the leaves give him peace,
May the hush of the forest receive him.
—Ezra Pound, "Prayer for a Dead Brother"

Beso Lifts His Nose

> *old friend what are you hearing*
> *that I do not hear though I listen*
> —W. S. Merwin

We welcome the wind
that traveled over the sea
and strawberry fields.
Beso's jaw stops working
for a moment as one ear
turns to the rustling sycamore
and the other to brittle leaves
spinning on the ground.
He lifts his nose to the west
and then raises it just
a little higher.

Beso's Dust

The wind touches
Beso's coat.

Earth is a donkey
rigged to carry everything
until everything dies.

Then it will carry dust,
Beso's dust,
whirling in the wind

if there is wind.

Silence Beso

We encounter clean skulls
in surrounding hills and fields.
Only Beso knows
what he makes of them
as he sniffs out fodder
and I try to name the animal.
But it's always the same one—
silence.

Beso Huffed

I removed Beso's rigging
for the last time
but time keeps loading.

Today, a butterfly
landed on his withers
and Beso huffed.

Used Beso

He was in the pasture
resting his used body
under the blue oak.
Beso is tough and stoic
but today his eyes
seemed to speak
unspeakable sadness
when I disturbed sleep
more valuable to him
than two Fuji apples.

Beso

Beso stands under an eave
out of the rain,
head down,
as if he hopes the cargo master
will pass him by.
Tired, ears flooded
with the sound of rain—
the starboard eye
half-closed.

Beso Keeps

Overcome by weariness,
Beso keeps to his stall.

One halfhearted ear tracks
hawks passing over the barn.

Beso's Question

To Beso, it is only
where heaven is—
good grass,
shade in summer,
sun in winter,
and the weightlessness
of sky.

Wall Beso

Beso stares at the barn wall.

He ignores my approach
appearing to be in deep
communion.

His tail hangs down like rope
from a hook.

Seeing Beso

Beso is silence
pouring itself into itself
without a song.

He sees through me
much farther than the moon
through water.

Soul Beso

An owl carries a mouse
in its talons

to the iron oak
on the hill.

Beso holds the moonlit
pasture.

Beyond Beso

The valley yields to evening
as if obeying the sign
at the crossroads.

Pastures keep to rules
of silence about the living
and the dead.

It is good to see the sun's
yellow being savored
by the clouds.

Nameless Beso

Names pour over
the ridge—
tide overspilling
moon.

Night alone
breathes in the pasture,
its many eyes
open.

Acknowledgments

"Attending Beso"

"**Unto all mortals let there be equal grace,** to pass from this life of agony by the gates of death into law; into the peaceful kingdom," from "Kumasaka," a Noh play in two Acts, by Ujinobu, reprinted in *Poems and Translations,* by Ezra Pound, (New York: The Library of America, 2003).

"I. Beso," Epigraph

"**I would have wished for you if I had known how** . . ." from "Little Horse," in *Migration,* by W. S. Merwin (Port Townsend, WA: Copper Canyon Press, 2005).

"Beso's Hooves"

"**And what with broken wheels and so on** . . ." from "Exiles Letter," by Rihaku (Li Po), in *Poems and Translations,* by Ezra Pound (New York: Library of America, 2003).

"Beso's Song"

" . . . **you built temples for them / in their hearing**," from *Sonnets to Orpheus* (No. 1), by Rainer Maria Rilke, translated by Edward Snow (New York: North Point Press, 2004).

"Cézanne and Beso"

"**It was said of Cézanne** . . ." from *Letters on Cézanne,* by

F

Rainer Maria Rilke, translated by Joel Agee (New York: North Point Press, 2002).

"Beso and His Peers"

"**An unapparent connexion is stronger than an apparent**," from *The Cosmic Fragments: A Critical Study with Introduction, Text and Translation,* by Heraclitus, translated by G. S. Kirk (London: Cambridge University Press, 1954).

"Al-Beso"

"**Zeus is never ridiculous, because his dignity is of no concern to him**," from *The Marriage of Cadmus and Harmony,* by Roberto Callasso (New York: Knopf, 1993).

"Equus Asinus, Beso—On Blame"

"**May terrifying winds carry off him / who blames me**," from "In My Pain," in *Sweetbitter Love: Poems of Sappho,* translated by Willis Barnstone (Boston: Shambhala, 2006).

"Beso Dozed Off"

" . . . **and tracking the wildfire** . . ." The Zaca Fire, Santa Barbara County, started July 4, 2007; 95% contained August 28, 2007; 240,207 acres.

"II. With Beso"

"**Mission: To be where I am** . . ." from "The Outpost," in *The Great Enigma: New Collected Poems,* by Tomas Tranströmer, translated by Robin Fulton New York: New Directions Press, 2006).

"Beso Brings Beso"

"There is one inside who walks like Jesus on the sea," from "The Ears," by Mevlana Jalaluddin Rumi, translated by Robert Bly, in *The Rumi Collection,* edited by Kabir Helminski (Boston: Shambhala, 2005).

"The Real Beso"

"A glass made of water / and full of water." "4" from *Vertical Poetry,* by Roberto Juarroz, translated by W. S Merwin (San Francisco: North Point Press, 1988).

"Beso Settles It"

"Inside my heart . . ." from "Withered Zen," in *Sun at Midnight,* by Muso Soseki, translated by W. S. Merwin and Soiku Shigematsu (San Francisco: North Point Press, 1989).

"Earthly Beso"

"Becomes one with the dusty world," from *Tao Te Ching,* Verse 4, by Lao Tzu, translated by Stephen Addiss and Stanley Lombardo (Indianapolis: Hackett Publishing Company, 1993).

"Beso Engages"

"You say nothing . . ." from "Asking The Rock That Holds UP MY Ch'in," in *The Selected Poems of Po Chu-I,* translated by David Hinton (New York: New Directions Press, 1999).

"III. Beyond Beso"

"May his soul walk under the larches of Paradise" from "Prayer for a Dead Brother," in *Poems and Translations,* by Ezra Pound (New York: The Library of America, 2003).

"Beso Lifts His Nose"

"old friend what are you hearing . . ." from "To Maoli as the Year Ends," in *Migration,* by W. S. Merwin (Port Townsend, WA: Copper Canyon Press).

About the Author

RICHARD JARRETTE is a psychotherapist with nearly forty years experience specializing in abused, damaged, and neglected adults, teenagers, and children. He directed an alcohol and drug recovery treatment center as well as a counseling center adjacent to San Quentin State Prison for families of inmates. Jarrette attended USC–UCLA and The Fielding Institute and holds degrees in clinical psychology and English. While in college he came across the poem "Little Horse," by W. S. Merwin, in a chapbook entitled, *Animae* and immediately knew that this was a kind of response to Ezra Pound's "Personae," and the poem's impact on his life was incalculable. *Beso the Donkey* may be a response to or dialogue with this poem forty years later. Jarrette has written a screenplay, *Better Stuff,* and continues to write poetry.